Machines on the Road

S....

Raintree

Raintree is an imprint of Capstone Global Library Limited,
a company incorporated in England and Wales having its
registered office at 7 Pilgrim Street, London, EC4V 6LB –
Registered company number: 6695582

www.raintreepublishers.co.uk
myorders@raintreepublishers.co.uk

Text © Capstone Global Library Limited 2014
First published in hardback in 2014
Paperback edition first published in 2015
The moral rights of the proprietor have been asserted.

Edited by Dan Nunn and John-Paul Wilkins
Designed by Cynthia Akiyoshi
Picture research by Elizabeth Alexander
Production by Helen McCreath
Originated by Capstone Global Library Ltd
Printed and bound in China by Leo Paper Products Ltd

ISBN 978 1 406 25939 1 (hardback)
17 16 15 14 13
10 9 8 7 6 5 4 3 2 1

ISBN 978 1 406 25944 5 (paperback)
18 17 16 15 14
10 9 8 7 6 5 4 3 2 1

British Library Cataloguing in Publication Data
Smith, Siân.
Machines on the road. – (Machines at work)
388.3'2-dc23
A full catalogue record for this book is available from the
British Library.

Acknowledgements
We would like to thank the following for permission to
reproduce photographs: Alamy pp. 8 (© david pearson),
10 (© Ian Pilbeam), 13 (© South West Images Scotland),
18 (© Dan Callister), 21 (© Alvey & Towers Picture
Library); Corbis p. 12 (© donna day/Big Cheese Photo);
Shutterstock pp. 4 (© 1000 Words), 5, 14,15, 23 cab, 23
trailer (© Vibrant Image Studio), 6, title page (© oksana.
perkins), 7 (© Lebedev Maksim), 9 (© Ivan Cholakov),
16 (© Baloncici), 17 (© formiktopus), 19 (© Pawel
Nawrot), 20 (© Mike Brake), 22 (© Dmitry Kalinovsky),
23 deck (© James Steidl), 23 fuel (© Concept Photo), 23
pollution (© M. Shcherbyna), 23 siren (© Ilya Andriyanov);
SuperStock pp. 11, 23 tracks (© Manfred Segerer/
image/imagebroker.net).

Design element photographs of car engine part (©
fuyu liu), road texture (© PhotoHouse), and gear cog (©
Leremy) reproduced with permission of Shutterstock.

Front cover photograph of sports car reproduced with
permission of SuperStock (Transtock). Back cover
photographs of road sweeper (© Baloncici) and lorry (©
Vibrant Image Studio) reproduced with permission of
Shutterstock.

We would like to thank Dee Reid and Marla Conn for their
invaluable help in the preparation of this book.

Every effort has been made to contact copyright holders
of material reproduced in this book. Any omissions will be
rectified in subsequent printings if notice is given to the
publisher.

Contents

Some words are shown in bold, **like this**. You can find out what they mean by looking in the glossary.

Why do we have machines on the road?

People make machines to do different jobs.

Machines on the road help people to travel quickly and easily.

Some machines can carry lots of people, animals, or things.

Other machines make roads clean and safe for everyone to use.

What types of car can you see on the road?

There are many different types of car, but they are all used to help people travel.

Sports cars are made to move fast.

sports car

tyres

Some cars are made to move over bumpy and muddy roads.

These powerful cars can have big tyres.

Most cars use petrol or diesel **fuel** to make them move.

Some cars use vegetable oil, gases, or electricity instead. This makes less **pollution**.

electric car

limousine

Some rich or famous people travel in limousines with special windows.

People inside can look out of the windows, but anyone outside cannot see in.

Which other machines carry people?

Buses and coaches are made to carry lots of people.

Some buses have two **decks** or are long and bendy to fit more people in.

tram

tracks

Trams are also used to carry lots of people.

Trams move along **tracks**, just like a train.

Why are bicycles and motorbikes useful?

Bicycles are useful for short trips because they do not need any **fuel**.

Tandem bicycles can carry two people at once.

tandem

Motorbikes are small and fast.

They can help police officers to get through traffic and reach places quickly.

What are the biggest machines on the road?

The biggest road machines are lorries. They can carry huge loads.

Many lorries have a bed in the **cab**, where drivers can sleep on long journeys.

cab

trailer

Lorries and the **trailers** they pull have many wheels.

They need lots of wheels to carry the weight of the lorry and its load.

Which machines help to clean the roads?

Machines called road sweepers use brushes to clean up dirt and rubbish.

Some spray water. Some can blow out air and suck up dirt like a vacuum cleaner.

Bin lorries also collect rubbish.

Machines on these lorries can lift up bins and squash rubbish to make it smaller.

Which road machines help to keep us safe?

Police cars, fire engines, and ambulances are used to keep people safe.

Their flashing lights and **sirens** help them to travel quickly, by telling people to move out of the way.

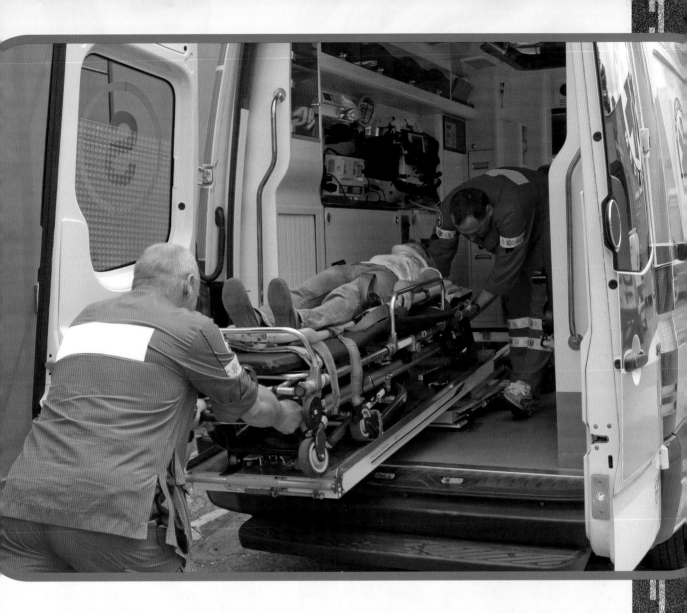

Ambulances are used to take people to hospital when they are ill or hurt.

A bed can fit in the back and there are special machines to help people.

Firefighters put out fires by using long hoses on fire engines.

A machine in the fire engine controls how much water comes out of each hose.

hose

snow plough

Other machines make roads safe by getting rid of ice and snow.

Snow ploughs are used to push away snow. Machines that spread salt help to melt ice.

21

What does this road machine do?

Can you guess what this machine does?

Find the answer on page 24.

Picture glossary

 **cab** place where the driver sits

 **deck** a floor or level. Some buses can have two floors or decks.

 **fuel** something we put into cars and other vehicles to make them go

 **pollution** harmful dirt or gases that can damage the world around us

 **siren** machine that makes a loud hooting or wailing noise.

 **tracks** metal lines or rails that trains and trams move along

 **trailer** container or holder on wheels that is pulled along

23

Find out more

Books

Big Book of Big Machines, Minna Lacey
   (Usborne Publishing, 2010)
On the Road (Machines Rule), Steve Parker
   (Franklin Watts, 2012)

Website

www.topgearturbo.com/games/
Play car challenges from the popular BBC
television series.

Index

The road machine on page 22 is a steamroller.
It is used to make roads flat and even.